SINGING BONE

SINGING BONE

KATHARINE BITNEY

© 1997, Katharine Bitney

All rights reserved. No part of this book may be reproduced, stored in a retrieval system or transmitted in any form or by any means without written permission from The Muses' Company, an imprint of J. Gordon Shillingford Publishing Inc., except for brief excerpts used in critical reviews.

The Muses' Company Series Editor: Catherine Hunter
Cover design by Terry Gallagher/Doowah Design
Author photo by Debra Mosher
Cover photograph of 45,000 year old flute made from bone. Photo by Srdjan Zivuloviv. Used with permission of Archive Photos/Reuters.

Published with the assistance of The Canada Council for the Arts.

Printed and bound in Canada

Some of these poems have appeared in *Dandelion,*
Prairie Fire, CV2, New Quarterly and *Grain*

Canadian Cataloguing in Publication Data

Bitney, Katharine
 Singing bone

ISBN 1-896239-22-6

 I. Title.

PS8553.I8776S55 1997   C811'.54   C97-900239-7
PR9199.3.B456S55 1997

To Athena

*Thanks to the Manitoba Arts Council
for a grant to begin work on this manuscript.*

*Thanks to Catherine Hunter for asking for the book,
and for her diligent work as Editor.*

*Thanks to Anne Szumigalski for
her vital help and commentary.*

*Thanks to Lynne Mitchell-Pedersen for her impassioned
explanation as to why I have to keep on writing poems.*

*Thanks to Frances for never
ceasing to make fun of me.*

Thanks to Andris for unfailing support.

Contents

Mother of Dream

You Couldn't Find Me / 13
The Names of Sleep / 14
The Night Shift / 15
When You Can't Sleep / 16
Dreamed of 2010 / 17
Have I Been Dreaming / 18
La Force / 19
Even As We Speak / 20
Gifts / 21
Dreams of Succulents and Mice / 22
The Glance: After a Painting / 23
The Door Out / 24
Double Dreams / 25

Bone Flute

Woman/Bone Flute/The Theory of Music / 29
About the Goddess / 30
The Wedding / 31
Terns / 32
The Garden / 33
Voice of the Blue Harpsichord / 39
The Notes Are Pregnant / 40
Vivaldi / 41
Snowstorm in Four Movements / 42
The Fuguist / 43
At the Lake in November / 44

The Risk

This is a Fight / 47
Regarding the Stars / 48
Because in Space / 49
The Dance / 50
These Bodies / 51
Bodybuilding / 52
Rain and What It Means / 53
Committed to the Flight / 55
Going to the Wall / 56
Cups and Swords / 57
Across the Bering Strait / 58
Inner Geometry / 59
Need to Know / 60
Word / 61
Minton / 62
Remembering How As a Child
You Were Fearless / 63

Around the Women's Fire

The Transformer: A Song / 67
Fall Wind / 68
Anatole Goes to Church / 69
Hatshepsut / 70
Eight Fires / 71
A Winter Solstice Altar:
Mary Waits for the Child to Be Born / 72
A Gnostic Poem / 73
I Build an Altar / 74
The High Place at Megiddo / 75
The Operating Table / 76
A Prayer for Vernal Equinox / 77
Praise / 78
Around the Women's Fire / 79
Grandma's Stone / 80
Everything I Knew / 81
The Fire in Her Hands / 83

If I build a poem out of bones
how will I choose   with what shall I begin
With the jawbone of T-Rex   the skull of an ox
a bison   with the shell of a nautilus
Will I choose the armbone of an ancestor
and who should she be   Was she buried in a coffin
was she tossed excarnate on a midden heap
and should I write on that bone my life story

MOTHER OF DREAM

You Couldn't Find Me

You couldn't find me because I was sleeping   I tell you this so you know next time   if you can't find me I'm sleeping   And this might be in the afternoon   I'll have gone somewhere without you but don't be frightened   I haven't died   just fallen asleep for awhile   I may be on the couch or I may be on a beach in a willow thicket on the white dunes   half listening to the waves   to the shouts of bathers   boaters   to the screams of gulls   In my sleep I see pelicans   their silent flight and the concert of feeding   All birds dive at once to scoop up fish in their pouches   And who knows where they nest   somewhere along the shore

The Names of Sleep

Son of Morpheus
Daughter of Death
Mother of dream
Father of restoration
Cousin of winter

that knits the ravelled sleeve
that leads you away from day
that makes you sweat in the sun
that makes your cheeks rosy in winter
that escorts babies gently into the world
the dying gently out

there is the sleep of angels
the sleep of the just
the sleep in the arms of the father
the sleep in the bosom of Abraham

here's where the body is refreshed
where cells renew themselves
where molecules silence the mind
where silencing the mind molecules speak to each other
over clear telephone wires
the static of movement quieted

here in the enormous universe of the body
in the laboratory of the body molecules advise the mind
the mind lies back and lets them do their work
closes its eyes and watches particles cha cha

the body forgets it will be stiff in the morning
limbs in dream chasing   being chased
running away   flying   riding horses

The Night Shift

We have no home   Call us fireflies   the atoms that haunt you when you sleep   Fireflies because you think you can see us in your half-sleep   pins of light at the edge of vision   Or dancing in the 3D theatre of your inner eye   the inside of your eyelids   Here's where we go to work just as the sun goes down and you think you hear night rain   It's us   We're on the job with our lunch buckets under one arm   our tool kits under the other   Some call us spies   some busybodies   even sleepydust   Well let them call us what they like   we're not fools or children   Every generation has seen us since man stood upright on the savannahs   noticed that night is beautiful   that beauty is dangerous   We are merely the dust motes of dreams   the stuff that movies are made of   Don't take it personally either   it's just a job like any other   We could as easily coalesce into granite or paper or some part of your body   the liver   say

When You Can't Sleep

When you can't sleep too warm too close to the open throat of music every atom of you agitated   singing singing in the middle of the night

All nightbirds   throats open   your molecules listen and sing listen and sing   drown out the druggy voice of sleep   every atom every quark of you alert for the cough of the saber tooth the opera of wolves

All night   past three   past four   your body buzzes against the bed neon against glass   breeds irritable light   you can blame impressionable genes in you the ancient chromosomes of hominids still jiggle with fear of fiery eyes   of voices in the dark

Until your bones ache and sing in their sheath of skin   you toss and turn in the skin of night   listen for the late train's long recitative

Perhaps it's the long season straining against change   your body reaching for it   late leaves rise from the ground   a school of fish   a flock of plovers   whirl   settle on tiny oceans of lawn

Dreamed of 2010

Dreamed of 2010   the Joker
the computer   moons of Jupiter
the long journey
getting the hang of it
looking out the window of the ship
seeing a satellite
Neptune passing

you can't fall off   fall down in space
I was getting the hang of it
the Joker walks on nothing
spacewalk is a cakewalk
is this part of the dream

Have I Been Dreaming

as usual I lie down under an aspen   evenings   or nights   even afternoons when the sun floods down   beats hard on you like an angry woman or child so you wake up sweaty and headachy   have I been dreaming again   the patter of leaves the swish of wind in the top branches   did I dream the girl swimming far out in the lake the water around her a platinum pool   you can see her mouth work saying or singing something that hits the water   chips the waves with light   what is it she says   do I dream she calls someone on the shore   an animal perhaps or a tree   the motor boats drown out her voice and their wake waves break up the sun on the lake surface

La Force

Five AM   I dreamed again of the lion man
the soft cleft of his cat mouth and how will she kiss it
and how he knows the moon is an ornament of love

I dream of the lion and the woman
this embrace as easy as her hands resting on his face
she leans down with her angel hands and he doesn't move
she reaches into the cat lip with her tongue

Even As We Speak

Even as we speak sleep rages in someone's brain   it's a distant hope a shore that keeps moving away as the ship of the mind sails toward it

How sad you say when people fail to slip down into that darkness that light   but I tell you even as we speak someone stares out the night window   watches trees not moving in no wind   and listens for the sound of no cars on the neon-shined street   the rain-slicked road   such nights are for people like us who turn them into movies   poems   songs   the sad guitar strings shuffled by tired lovers' fingers   the girl/the boy still sleeping on the mattress   on the bed pale green streetlight shines in and the unsleeping lover at the tall window   head in hands   thinks the night will go on like this forever   the fever of sleep raging in the brain

And while we sit here talking you can be sure there is a fool on every boulevard gazing at the night   the television   or hard at work in a studio painting out the nightmares trapped in her furious mind   she slaps on colours   waits for the lover to come back   wake up   for companionship   a drink   a cigarette

And the lover on the mattress how can he sleep how can he turn away like that just gallop off into another dimension as though this one doesn't exist except as a place to leave the body   for even as we speak the spirits of a million sleepers rise up   flee

Gifts

All night we lay on our backs out in the stars
floating   still there as outlines if you look
white outlines in the blue
all night we pulled in matter
filled our bodies   the cores
of stars   planets   asteroids
it was hiding presents on Christmas Eve
waking we'll watch the entrepreneurs
in their rough ships sniff out our gifts
follow the opulent trail out the galaxy

Dreams of Succulents and Mice

Horses eat daisy dreams
mole rats eat the dreams of succulents
plant dreams of Africa
who is still a maiden in the kopjes

dreams of water dreams
of brilliant flowers
plants inventing themselves
feeding their fantasies to god

mice suck dreams from fleshy leaves
beetles from the flowers
take them down
into the lazy underground

such drama as the plants sleep
their charged dreams
change place   explode

The Glance: After a Painting

girl of the jungle   the grasslands   paper shadow   face of the ages of man   eyes curious/frightened   peer through paper trees/people   tissue ghosts   things dried from age   pressed flowers   carcasses

she's bigger than a movie goddess on a giant screen   man only a shadow in her dream   she scries the future   dried fish twisting in arctic wind

side to side she moves her eyes   whatever you want to see in them looks out   the glance   every curve of earth in her white eyes

the girl runs pellmell through the trees   ferns brush her knees dire wolf stalks at her heels

The Door Out

And when you dream like that   the days collapsed the nights a jumble   do you ache for insomnia to shut those horrors out   do you beg for release   to wake up in the real world where death is not a joke   where suffering is not mocked   you must tell me   does relief flood you as you wake up deep in the night   the search those hot dreams   and do you wish for no sleep at all   to walk the floor half watching an old movie flicker on tv   half watching the night outside go on and on   the assurance of descending snow   of cold stars clanging in the sky   and when you bang awake having dreamed like that   do you search for the catalyst   too much cake too much fruit soda before bed   but knowing knowing all along the door out is next to the dream

Double Dreams

Now wouldn't you know it we're back in the same old dream again just the two of us back to back in the queen-sized bed   How odd then that quite the opposite to sleep is happening   Hand in hand we go into the dream   On the bed our bodies twitch   grind their teeth   twist in the blankets   The room is too small for the world we enter hand in hand back to back to the same old dream

And when you think about it doesn't it seem strange we hardly notice the world outside our bedroom window   The promised storm shies away   moves on   Was it us   did we frighten it   Those tall clouds those towering thunderheads back off not daring to boom at our sleep when we dream together

Some night we won't do this   dream together   Some night it will be just me or just you walking off into a separate dream and the other will sit reading or get up and walk round the night garden braving mosquitoes   will stand under the apple tree on the lawn now silver with moon   and turn away to other considerations   how not to be alone for instance

Bone Flute

Woman/Bone Flute/The Theory of Music

Creating Eve god makes a mistake   because the number of bones on each side of Adam's ribcage is uneven   So god takes a rib from the other side and makes of it a flute   And this he gives to the woman   What is it for   asks the woman   Use your imagination   says god or god says nothing

So after they get kicked out of paradise the man and woman go on a journey   They come to a cliff edge   And the woman keeps on walking The man says where are you going   Across says the woman   The man laughs   You can't go across there   you'll fall   That's what you think   says the woman   And she blows her bone flute   And note by note a bridge appears spanning the chasm   and together they walk across   Of course the man envies the woman her flute   He wants it for himself

One night he waits until the woman is asleep then creeps to her side and lays his hand on her flute   But it burns him with a terrible fire so he screams and rolls away   He puts his hand in the river to cool it   A great steam arises and rolls in over the land   a thick fog   The woman wakes up   sees what has happened   cries out   Give me back my flute   The man cries back   give me back my bone

The man and woman continue their journey walking across the world   talking   arguing   the man still seething with envy and rage   The woman sees this but says nothing because she and the flute are made out of the man's body   because they were created and taken by god

Their shouting rises   falls   a chant   the high voice of the woman   the low voice of the man   this song   the tension and harmony between their voices   and god thinks   yeah   not bad

About the Goddess

I can't tell you a thing about the goddess   I've never met her only glimpsed her on the horizon of history   of other people's minds   You and I might walk together toward those horizons   find there nothing but debris   statues broken and torn down   and her just a pile of rubble in the grass   Where to begin?   With Eve?   With Lilith?   Gaia?

Eve then as she slides through the deep grass of Eden   sifts the possibilities of being free   a god   of seeing   through a glass darkly yes but seeing   choosing   Is it now perhaps that she pulls out her flute   the one god gave her   and sits down on a tuffet under a tree and the serpent loops cosily by her feet smiling up at her   does she play for him and he does he rise up on his coils and dance for her   swaying as her tunes ascend   the notes roosting in the branches of the tree   Does he sing as well as dance   does he doff his top hat and if god or Adam happens by and sees them together does Eve laugh and brush it off saying   Oh him   he's just a friend

Adam of course being frightened might say   Yes him   Can't you see he's just a snake in the grass   And Eve saying   Oh but he's so pretty

Well now what do you think   Is Eve a goddess?   Isis for instance used a serpent to wrest from old Ra his secret name   Was that what Eve was after and did she ever decode the Tetragrammaton?   Was she this close and Yahweh panicked   throwing her and her wimpy mate out of paradise?   And Yahweh's tantrum   did Eve secretly laugh at him for it and was he wise enough to understand?

The Wedding

Before they were born   the bride and groom resolved to carry on the fight   into a new world through the future as far as they could see all through their lives down time the fight was everything the standoffs   the passionate reunions   the flight across prairie down to the eastern sea

Now as the priest renews their vows thunder claps and the downpour drums like soldiers' boots on the church roof   spoiling their photos soiling the bottom of her gown   In the decorated car she scowls at him   Our life will be like this   she says   dark clouds quick storms   the hope of intermittent sun   Have you forgotten the groom replies   us tumbling down centuries until you give me back my bone   Ha says the bride just you try and take it

At the feast the bride stands up at the head table   pulls her flute out of thin air and plays   The song charms even the angry groom He vows to carry on the fight   for that song   for seeing her in the forest hair tied back in a checkered kerchief   knowing the name of every plant   the arrangement of fossils under every biome for her bending down at the beach a starfish in each hand   her flute sticking out the back pocket of her jeans

In the hotel   he reaches for her arm   leads her to dance   The floor is all waving bodies   grain or kelp in the wind the sea of music

Terns

...float on the backs of tiny winds a bird's eye view of the lagoon down in the eelgrass fish flash silver   pole to pole beaches are the same to the tern   white sand the world over   black cliffs white with guano

down the beach an angry woman plays a flute the tern thinks it looks like whalebone or dinosaur bone   but intent on silver flashing through the sea   moves his eyes from the woman swoops down snatches the struggling fish the woman doesn't need to look there is a white translucent angel hovering between her and the sun its little eyes are black holes   the woman anchors herself to earth with a tune

The Garden

1.

One day I'm dug up in someone's garden
a small tea-coloured skull with pronounced sagittal crest
and two false teeth   The gardener scoops it up

He mounts my mottled head on a pitchfork
I watch him dig   I tell him
take my hipbone for a spade
The baffled gardener does as he is told
afraid I'll come back to life   replace him
Because you've gardened up my grave   I say
I'll tell you what I know
about the apple tree   the rose   about lettuce
the tulips I used to grow

My skeleton clatters to the ground   crosses its legs
folds its hands   its tea-coloured bones
I chatter on   Now take a rib
and make of it a flute
as you blow it will speak
all the poems I didn't have time to write
old fugues   equations
I promise to be quiet

The gardener plays my missing rib to his plants
partitas of Bach
peasant songs of the Andes
To keep time I rattle my neck   which in life was short
I love him now

The concert done   my pelvis returns to spading the dirt
my skull   back on the fence   issues instructions tells stories
singing   singing the livelong day

2.

Polonaise

Babcia lifts the cherry branches
into a pitcher   thin cream
of light pours in through the window
settles in a pool around her hands

Nocturne

the living goddess twists her wrist
a dainty move   a tiny branch
slides down the china throat
geodesic curves spray up
against the downward Himalayas

Etude

into a crystal vase my hands lance
thin boughs of cherry blossoms
pale as Chopin
this evening's delicate étude
the sun is éclatant
its slant isosceles
map of a homeland

3.

Spring is all green verbs
light cones   apple tree
a geodesic in full fleece
bowed arms holding bowls
of popcorn flowers
curves within curves

Wind shakes petals
down umbrella boughs
parabolas   and a halfcircle
over the dome of earth

Under the apple tree
time runs round itself
in a fairy ring
gathering probabilities
the perfect sphere
seems to need more

4.

I come back to the apple tree
the cherry bush
the shade under them and the cat
sleeping in the drug of blossoms
tulips engineered to look like parrots   peonies
herbs like the mystic rue just another plant
the flax   its small blue flowers the eyes of god
looking out then closing

5.

Out there   theft of life is a regular event
the magpie garden thieving
that shiny thing   water
caught on a web
in the fleurets of a dill plant

The shock the fall from the tower
the little pomes that form on apple trees
tiny pomes which will become apples
little apples with blushed cheeks

6.

Since death   my father misses
the great canon of seasons
the themes and variations
he's with me now   dreaming
the air velvet around trees

Everything gardened
this artificial landscape turns fauve
the light wind mauve from the scent of lilac

All the family's memories ride
on the back of this soporific wind
that blows through the house in summer

7.

full bloom begins to rot around the edges   hollyhock   the headache
plant   huge   high as the upstairs window   black   red   lavender
white   white with pink faces   slouches   watches little murders
in the foliage   the bodies buried in dry soil for later
resurrection   seeds eggs pupae nymphs curled in their hard
sarcophagi   webs chrysalises seed shells egg cases   socked away
into branches and under the great warm corpses of decaying plants

in the garden as on the steppe everything in its place   a place
for everything   fall and spring the gardener turns the soil turns
up the bones of last year's crops   the bodies fly out
burst into air

8.

He watched the season fall
leaves driven down by wind
heard Palestrina
opening the vaults of sky

He watched   the sky performed
rise/fall rise/fall
the birds were quarks
migrating geese   a wedge of mercy
the hymn was gamma rays
blessings to fallen leaves
on lawns   fruit rotting

and the world sang gloria gloria
the garden torn up by its roots
the turned soil drinking cosmic rain

He watched   the world
which was his garden fled
in waves disappearing
into leaves
driven down by wind

9.

the zodiacs arise
their wheels spiral in twilight
day plundered by night
roundness of night

we feel our way by the roundness of pillars
what tiny shafts of light slide in
from what moon there may be
strike the pictures   hippopotamus
falcon's beak
stylus of Thoth   an ankh

the light is birds   they flit
from glyph to glyph
we read them in sequence as the light leads us
prophecy   revelation
your soul standing at your shoulder
evenings   especially the cool ones   yes

in the night garden a man unbinds his favourite tree
he takes a strand of the swaddling   circles
unwraps the corpse for resurrection

Voice of the Blue Harpsichord

Taking the night wind   birds lift off
from the bay   they fly at the moon
covering with their wings that old goddess
naked again and full

she sits at the blue harpsichord
pushes down keys
the notes rise up   in twos   threes
then all at once   the chords break
into songs   arpeggios
a flock of night birds calling
taking off into the wind

The Notes Are Pregnant

Pregnant with embellishment   notes
waddle up the stave   holding their backs
a great fat halfnote   hardly able to move
takes a rest
the next step impossible
how stupid they look   they all feel

far too many to a bar
once they've let loose their progeny
it reminds the listener of a clothesline
littered with squabbling crows

Vivaldi

flowers tucked in her wimple the nun conducts an all-girl orchestra white and garlanded   their bows slide over the strings of their violins violas

Master Vivaldi listens from the balcony   watches through the wooden grate   oh girls with flowers in your hair   the sunshine slides through the windows warming your hands lighting your young faces solemn with the business of making music together   every note noted every possible note played

these are angels who play his music   his body is all the cellos held between their young knees   his head all the violins resting on their shoulders   Vivaldi's hands slide up their dresses   caress their silky legs as they play

Snowstorm in Four Movements

I wrote that blizzard
one boring winter afternoon
the harpsichord empty of song
the music room altogether too peaceful

so   first   the long waltz down
snow in three-four time
glittering ballgowns
white tuxedos
sequins   rhinestones   pearls

then   presto   wind shredding cloud
white typhoons
tear off your clothes
howl at the window
rip your breath away
shoot bullets at your feet
to make you jig

sure I did it
why shouldn't I
you were getting stupid with repose
no spring in your step
so here's to the orage
allegro furioso

and here's to the aftermath
the dancers panting on the floor
the orchestra spent
music piled up in drifts
against the door

The Fuguist

Number One winds round itself
oooo's nothings   Lacunar integer
behind itself all the way
sings its own sweet song
dividing contrapuntally
breaks down into decimals   dreamstates
always in the present tense
largo fugato

So out steps Number Two
leaves One a sleeping shell
the lulled subject of a self-created trance
Two thinks One is a fool
(such solipsism) and says so
The psychiatrist is impressed

Two begins to prophesy
Instead of words   out of Two's mouth
unsolvable equations pour   complicated songs
fill up the air

This episode calls for an answer
the subject calls for an answer
gets back countersubject
dry as a bone

At the Lake in November

1.

The howling lake   crash of ice as it freezes
sounds like   a train derailing
like   a spitfire howling down the sky
like howler monkeys   ice moans
heaves up pentagons hexagons dodecahedrons
the waves freeze in place   crested   splashed on shore

Now the sky at night   how do you explain such blackness
such a plethora of lights   how in morning
the mystery of wolf tracks   how they got there without
your seeing   lake howls like a demon day and night

2.

But all this silence
but the silence
But because the silence
Because the silence becomes but
the silence this becomes all
but the silence

the blue silence the white
the silence

The Risk

This is a Fight

This is a fight against death   push push push against water through water   pulse of our tiny bodies in the sea   Against death we push sea water through flimsy bodies   all gel and skeleton   all light and sea salt   What a deal   What a mandate   Push push push into time   the water your god   your enemy   I'll be a coelacanth you a whale shark   We're the vanguard   baleen and krill   those floppy things in the sea   Push push   the sea too big the land too small   Push push   no safety   What's in it for us   Push push   this fight against death

And if we stay here   fight for our lives   a moment of light   the future mirrored in the sea swim swim   what's in it for us   just plankton seeing the future deep in the heaving sea

Who told us   who made us swim and push for our lives   who said push push push   swim   survive?   Who said?   Who said?

Regarding the Stars

Regarding the billions of stars
happy in their red lives   white lives
those dervish worlds   dustbowls   molten balls
the one red eye   the big blue hurricane

we in our tiny bodies   suited up for life
heavy with terrestrial gods
try to move out there

called up from the spirit world
we go as ghosts
fly through lattices of matter
cut through the red tape of spacetime
our minds free of it

And where else in the universe
is there life like this
carbon burning itself to ash

Because in Space

Because in cold space
there is no gravity
you among the stars merely tumble
gymnast spreadeagled
over a painted backdrop
no longer sky

you put your mind to it
in spite of yourself
pull everything into place
particles into atoms
atoms into molecules
molecules into all manner of things

because this is how god does it
raids daydreams for fireweed
apple tree   snow   city   farm
paring knife   cabbage
everything imagines itself
scenarios invented on the run
things rush past themselves
stop only to coalesce   fly on

no time for a lunch break here
not in cold space
where warehoused seasons lie
inside each other

actors in the green room
self bumps into self
costumed   preening
practising lines
straining to hear cues
the chorus

The Dance

a snake of human bodies winds
down to the streets of Rio
their dancing shoes make rags of their ankles

this is the dance between lives
you try on costumes of a hundred ages
dance till the spirit floats
flops down exhausted on midnight lawns
the carnival everywhere around you

These Bodies

1.

these bodies are fog   fume
shadows and caricatures
small heroes   ghosts   carcasses
hanging in closets   in a meat locker
all flim flam   Superman   Rambo
these bodies are tissue paper
all flammable   all bowing
to Madonna   to Marilyn Monroe

2.

these shadows blow shofars
growing from their mouths
or phalluses entering
or children being eaten
or prophecies coming out
this world was offered life three times
and twice refused it

3.

before there were people
spectres walked the earth
their feet   made of light
floated   not touching
they were aliens   angels   architects

of the world to come
of the way evening light will blanket skyscrapers
blinding their glass eyes
the way vehicles will move one way down a street
and people another
trees will cast their pleasing shadow
clouds disperse over cities

Bodybuilding

This is the realm of air
your body a swarm of atomic bees
like lovers the elegant machines move you
smooth your edges
fill you with grace
the radio jogs you along
you feel like a million bucks
no to the inches   no to the fat
jock girls in t-shirts   stretch shorts

Air through arms   legs
air swimming through eyes
bodybuilding ladies
air air air
garbage and air

Rain and What it Means

1.

Inside angels and men are engrams
hardened on the page   encoded
every particle an actor
just add water   add light
Inside the gods are dots on microfilm
for poet spies   priest spies
who reach in
pull out the theatre

2.

Fool   who are you
you are the risk I take
there go the daredevils
cycling up thin wires to the sky
there go the jugglers
balancing clay pots
on their sagittal crests
small parasols are wings
that sway and arc above the world
lifting the acrobats
to the high wires of heaven

3.

this is not a poem
this is fear extruding on a screen
this is Mozart tickling the nerves
head full of hot air floats
on willy-nilly wind

a fugue
a tangle
a fight
don't worry about it
move along   move along   move along

the great orange of the soul
devises selves
pips turned outward

4.

Now go down   go back to the world
the beginning if there is a
beginning is the centre of a jewel
is the light in the centre of the jewel
the idea   the energy that sends the idea
outward

5.

grey sky down to the ground
the water
       look inside
       don't give me platitudes
       give me energy

passes   comes back in waves
tries to move my hands
but I am in the wheel
can't help that boys   here I am
words come out backwards

Committed to the Flight

What did you think it would be
Riding in an airplane
you can't get out till it lands
you sit   wait
can only imagine the relief
when you land safely
You live for this

First you get in
strap in
the plane begins to taxi
you are committed to the flight

It lifts off
climbs
flies bumps shivers
you drink something strong
finally the plane descends

bounces along another runway   halts
you stand   reach for your coat   purse
the book you couldn't bring yourself to read
You get off
swearing never to fly again

Going to the Wall

the last time we floated here
waiting for the sea to calm
our ship of surrogates was off to war
in a place we'd never heard of
brother   twin
counterpart   another
would become soldier   nurse
and us in the ship   souls waiting
to take their places in the old world
heroes come home

the last time we floated here
our sails wide open   prow cleaving water
sending up curls of spray to the other world
our boat was a merchant ship
bloated with pottery
the blue   the green
fresh from the kilns

our boats are full of ghosts
old refugees staggering out of time
on the wild south seas

Cups and Swords

my house is on fire
pillars riddled into flutes
want to sprout
flames   songs   leaves

the pillars lean together
soldiers crossing a battlefield
gunfire bangs around them

crossed swords   pierced hearts
severed heads
bodies reel   fall down
grab for sticks   rods   wands
for transformation

as the din fades   peace
spirits hurry toward light
pause to pity corpses
abandoned on the killing field

our house is on fire
pillars are old guns
bodies   tipped cups
spilling on a farmer's field
battle noise segues into angel choirs
we the dead rise up   smiling

Across the Bering Strait

how our bones remind us of who we were
how the bones change   thicker here   thinner there
skulls moving forward and back   bigger   smaller
the thin cranium of homo sapiens sapiens

Had someone told me what it would be
I would have stayed unborn
Across unpeopled fields we float
everything around us tiny stars or stardust
the mothers weary with feeding children cold manna
the fathers weary with hope
this trek not what the gods ordered
or if they did   damn them
nothing to make shelters of but the cold

Now the hunt is part of our sleep
This is my dreamlife   smoking the moose hide
hands always busy   busy even at night
when light comes from fire and coal oil
when light comes in from the moon

Inner Geometry

1.

Why should I believe you   O Grand Geometer
those sacred shapes are everywhere
spirals   cylinders   spheres   wiggly lines
why should I pay attention when you pronounce
the inner geometry of all things
hexagon   hedron   dodecahedron
it's all mathematics to you all shape
all dna to you isn't it
crystals and ice
geometry of music
geometry of wind

2.

the soloist wanders among the tables
freezes the air with a gavotte
pours down fire and water
makes the air orderly
reveals its molecular structure
disco balls spinning slowly

3.

When Omar plays piano
this smoky bar becomes a place of fire
at the tables heads bend together
secret talks

Omar   in his evening suit   smiles
leans over the plunging keys
you think of trumpets   trombones
bright gold

Need to Know

1.

Take yourself to a distant spring
no hybrids   no big garden
just the scent of prairie
tundra   forest

Very well then let's get on with it
no bells   no temples   no money   no king
just shrouded prophecy
only what you need to know to live
Now try to tell a story
Try to explain infinity

2.

Yesterday   my sister brought me
wild flowers   grasses   a hundred blooms
with the odour of buckwheat honey in hot sun
I photographed them
will send you a print
This is how to save the world

Word

rose up from the ground as we walked   dust at our heels   it rose in the whirling dust the word leapt into mouths choked throats caked tongues it swung along with us   our swinging arms   the bones of the land disclosed it leapt into our open mouths we sang it spoke it rang down the sky   word filled us jangled the marrow of our bones rang down the line as we strode the desert kicking up dust it was word we tasted it filled it shaped our mouths   it was earth was rain it was manna   snow   it melted on our tongues   rose fell again day after day

Minton

1.

The road with its soft weedy spine passes a sweet marsh   The stands of dark bulrush sag   bounce with bird bodies   redwinged blackbirds their throaty trills released from the one bird self that clings to a hundred swaying rushes on the long marsh shores necklaced with sedge   mallard families   Light wind chips the water

Beyond the marsh nothing but one valiant tree   It struggles between the vague horizon and the enormous sky   defensive   heroic   a hermit Saint Francis holding birds beetles butterflies in its arms

This is a memory   a child on a sandy road walking barefoot in the ruts   taking for granted the softness of sand between toes   hot cold   as soft water   a blessing

2.

Each time I return it's changed again
and the people recall less and less
who went before   who moved away

I can't get past the slough
can't find the old house
everything bright   changed   halfeaten
the fields full of chemicals

and I try to explain to these strangers
this is where I lived
In this dream earth is heaved up
nothing remembers
me   reaching down the mud streets
for home

Remembering How As a Child You Were Fearless

1.

Listen to me   Get up and seize the morning
Jump down from the bed   Dress
Walk out the door
The miles are cool
Breezes wrap your bare legs
air is cushions or thin water
Go north on the dirt road
feels like sand
Over the hill there are monsters and evil men
Still   you are fearless
climbing the land in your pretty sandals
priestess   young lady warrior

2.

Proceed again toward the wan horizon
worrying not of war but smaller things
books   candles   children   streets
how to find a metaphor for love
the experiment is looser this time
chemical food   the price of education
the sky a cone pinned down
at the edges of earth's cerebral crown

so walking the girl begins her poem
mutters   chants to the listener reeds
the listener snipes and plovers
today's song should zing

AROUND THE WOMEN'S FIRE

The Transformer: A Song

you are the man
you lie down in the grass
long winter gone
short summer coming
you are the woman
in the short grass
you sleep

Willie Crow
walks out of the sea
walks into your sleep

Willie Crow   Willie Crow
plays a bone flute
blows life through a bone flute
mist through a bone flute
air through bone

tiny flowers white yellow blue
blown through a bone flute
drift in air
settle on the short grass
your hair

you are the man
you dream with Willie Crow
you are the woman
weaving mist
making a basket
making up a song

long winter gone
short summer coming
mist from a bone flute
dust from a drum

Fall Wind

1.

behold the horses   seeds flying on high wind
my herd streaming over the steppe
I ride the spume of clouds   princess on a swan
angel on horseback   mounting the great flat lands
old world belongs to me   princess on a white horse
princess on a swan   riding down the hill clouds
down canyons and the sea below
the steppe the sea of grass

2.

a man out of shadows wants to ride the white horse
the renegade   wide body curled to spring
nostrils churning out mist   his dance through sand
down mountains   out canyons   out the valleys on horseback
here is the lancer on his vaulting steed   here he comes again
wildeyed   urging the horse forward into the camera   into night
mountains   here is the hunter riding now the wolf at his side
the stallion rears at the blinding sun   the raised swords

Anatole Goes to Church

the tundra is a basilica
built on a holy place
a place of transformation

Anatole enters the cathedral
the bishop   singing Mass
grows a beak
lifting his arms in benediction
grows wings
his vestments turn into feathers
his staff a wand   a rattle
the sanctuary   fire on stone

all that he knows
shadow   ecstasy
the birdmen dancing
on the other side of the fire
women whose powers are in
drums and bone flutes
here is the bread   the wine
water and flesh

everything is greater than man
descent into past   the evil-smelling lodge
where they hold the rites

Hatshepsut

...dreams of other rivers
mountains   jungles
temples   cattle   leopards
dreams of pale people dressed in furs
living in snow
dreams of dogs
night sky ululating

The servant carries in my breakfast
on a bronze tray   dates   cold meat   wine
snow world melts into sunlight
the girl stands   naked and clean
fur wraps gone
she bends with the tray
sets it down on my table
bows   backs away to the door

~

Our pyramids are built with glittering caps
remembering something we have never seen
snow on mountains

~

On my tomb at least let them say I explored
and let them spell my name right

~

New worlds need portable gods
faceless   nameless
to be what you need them to be
our gods are too tied to the land

~

The long boat stays buried in the sand
mine to board and float away
down Kush   Zimbabwe
plough Africa forever
mark it with the languages
of other worlds

Eight Fires

Eight fires lick at the east   Wind pushes flames bow to the mountains
You can't tell sky from horizon   The woman sits apart   legs
crossed   arms loose in her lap   The battle will be for her

Hero lies naked on the sand   Old shaman chants   paints the man's body
with words   Every inch of the body covered   Each word a Necessity

What is the shaman writing?   Locusts hornets weasels poison snakes
invisibility   the names of chthonic gods   Except for his coat of
words Hero is naked   By morning even the soles of his feet are poems
even the palms of his hands his sword arm his lips are
spells   His torso is the history of the world since creation

What does the text do?   Deflect arrows?   Bend light?

Enemy sleeps on the other side of the mountains   He thinks of language
as a drum skin   He tightens it   tests it with his fingers
with the heel of his hand   O Mate Kali O Mate Durga   The song comes
in the sleep of the enemy   Hey Innana Ho Innana O Mate Kali O Mate
Durga   Oh what a wild tattoo   The words dance on the skin of the drum
They rise like dust around his jiving fingers   Like dust they fly away
On this day oh beautiful mother

What does the music do?   Change flesh to steel?   Push away air?

It is not for the woman to say how the fight will end   At dawn the men
become giants   rise up   big as gods   take up the whole horizon as men
will do   It's only another battle where there need be none   Even now she
hears the clang of words as Hero swaggers into view   Even now her scalp
hurts with anger as Enemy sings his battle song

They shout out her name   fall to   The shaman wrings his hands   anguished
The words may not hold the texts may be too old   O Mate Kali
O Mate Durga   Enemy sings and the light bends round him   Eight
fires leap from his mouth   Like tongues they eat the words from Hero's
body   lick him clean

Will he strike?   Who will win?   The woman yawns   Words words words
They fall from the sky as Enemy shouts his victory   They pour to
the ground as fallen Hero weeps   She gathers the words into her apron
tosses them among hazelnuts   On this day oh beautiful mother

A Winter Solstice Altar: Mary Waits for the Child to Be Born

(The Altar: A small cauldron in the snow, barbecue charcoals fueled with birthday candles circled with spruce and pine branches. Everything else is virgin snow, kneedeep, and a waxing moon in the black sky. The celebrants circle the altar and make a wheel of footprints in the snow.)

I put the Word in a pile of snow   I covered it with pine branches I let the Word cook under there I let the sun go down on it I let it cook in the dark

In the dark the Word took shape   At first it was a hum a tone   At first it was letters and sound   It didn't know yet what it would become You could see it as letters   Sometimes WORD sometimes LOGOS Sometimes it just said BABY   I had no power on it I could only sit and wait   knit the dark months away   knit the sky the sun bigger and bigger and the Word still growing in the dark

I would dream then that the Word was a child or the fetus of a wolf or the egg of a paper wasp   I would dream as I knit up the sky that the Word was a drop of water now solid now liquid now gas   I would dream it was nothing but action the thoughts of it zipping around nonspace   like peewee hockey players shooting around the puck of thought   colliding in mid ice   or like children on tricycles crashing together on sidewalks   in alleyways   the little vehicles flying their wheels spinning in midair

I knitted and waited   the little Word slept under the snow the pine branches   No use talking to it now except to soothe or explain the growing light

So it was me you spoke to when you came to dance on the snow   It was me to whom you gave that blessing   Let your labour not be too long let the child not be colicky   How kind of you   The Word may have heard you   The child may have thought it was a joke

A Gnostic Poem

I write to my sister: "I never could settle into the body—it was something foreign. Maybe the Greeks were right, the soul trapped in flesh, the Light trapped within you as though the flesh were dark were dark matter."

Then what are we doing dancing in the hills   dancing with flowers in our hair   what are we doing revelling in sex   what are we doing in our silks and cadillacs   what are we doing huddling down into the warm dark of sleep? Oh what are we doing sending our coloured dreams out to lie upon the earth   to hang in the turquoise sky? How could we?   To whom are we being false   to whom traitors?

I have nothing but questions for you God.   You who claim to know everything answer me this—why did you do it?

Perhaps I am asking the wrong question perhaps I shouldn't even ask. Fortunately you never answer anyway.

I build an altar   a place to put this body   to lay it down forever and if I turn away will it disappear   and if I return will it be eaten away like a piece of sky not there?

I Build an Altar

I build an altar   a pile of stones in a field   Everything I put on it is dead   flowers pulled from their stems   old bones   feathers dropped by a passing bird of prey   Bones of a squirrel   teeth of a saber tooth   teeth of an ancestor   What will this altar attract?   a little god of the dead?   spirits of animals?   the four elements?   the moon?

We stand in the meadow under the moon   circle the altar of bones and feathers the little pile of stones   We stand here waiting for the moon to come down   She wants blood   She always does

She drags it out of us   wants blood to flow down from a high place   an altar of rough hewn stones

Now you may ask why did we let her get away with it   the blood   the killing?   And I ask you has anything changed?   Find me a god who has no taste for blood

So I build an altar   a pile of stones on a hill   runnels down the four corners for the blood   a shovel and pail for the ashes

The High Place at Megiddo

We built an altar it was the centre of the world the universe the pouring out of light   This place was for blood flooding down stone runnels and into the web of soil

Someday they'll blame us for this holocaust on the high place   How many rams how many goats how many firstborn given to the gods and why don't they answer   But how could they know those squabblers what we were trying to say how we were trying to smite them to attention

So where do they live how can we get there   If we stand on the altar will we ascend to heaven   will their airships hover over Megiddo   beam us up to another world

How is it to be the priest the one who cuts all the throats the one with the blood-soaked robes   You repeat this exercise you repeat it almost daily the frightened lamb belled bleating struggling you hold it down with one hand and strike at its throat with the other   it holds you down with its eyes asking why as they film over close

And for a moment there is the rush as death happens   the lamb bleeds and shits and you set its corpse ablaze   The world smells of wool   blood   flesh   the smoke ascends   you could see it from miles around   You could smell it from heaven

And as the lamb dies the people sway their arms reaching upward the bells on their ankles ring as their feet crash the earth under them someone faints   The incense of death too strong

And someone in her heart says this is the blood of women the blood of life and she stands with her legs apart and her blood runs down the hill

The Operating Table

Only initiates are allowed into this holy of holies   The sacrifice struggles on the table   Quiet her! From above the plebeians watch their noses pressed against glass

Now the long knives shine on white linen arranged just so in ascending order   In the vestibule the celebrants have robed   green gowns   green caps   green masks so as not to contaminate the sacrifice   even with their holy breath   and gloves that fit like skin

This is a moveable altar   It is placed in the centre of the sanctuary   The sacrifice sleeps   her heart hooked to a monitor   her breathing pushes bellows up and down

A Prayer for Vernal Equinox

It doesn't really matter that the sun moves into Aries the old ram gods are dead as doorknobs now   sheep merely pasture beasts of the Antipodes   It doesn't matter that the Lamb of God is past his prime his seed collected   frozen for the future

And who could care less that Sol Invictus is just now passing the ancient moon   This puny star   that footling satellite   what are they laid up against Jupiter or the huge winnowing of the Milky Way   What god these days takes pride in balance   in the marriage of dark and light   What human cares that day is the equal of night

And what is earth this small blue world when you know the universe has no end there is no skin to it no outside only planets and planets and planets each one the apple of god's eye each one just a harem girl to some gigantic star   Oh what is the tipping of earth against the throb of quasars against the pulsing of galactic hives

Priests of astronomy   calculate for us the length of day the length of night   Look up with your radar telescopes   look up from your mountain towers   Let the clicking of your computers measure and measure and measure deep in your concrete bunkers underground

Praise

worlds collide just beneath the skin of seeing   tiny galaxies explode   alter everything just beneath perception   Too exciting for words and we can't see any of it   only the body   her light jiggling in our bones   her light the light of matter writhing in our bones

So her eyes like a bird's see in the dark   see collisions in the bones of matter   the bones of all planets   blood of all stars   plasma of light   the same light jumping in our bones the same the same the same

So her eyes   if they close   the universe goes out and her eyes are all that is left   lids closed down   the collisions the tiny worlds the atoms fly back into her mind sucked up into the nowhere of her mind   thus the universe comes and goes   her eyes open and close

Open and close and are we now in or out of her mind   are we in or out of her spiral body   which way shall we dance   she dance   wind or unwind   breathe in   breathe out

The birds of her mind loop back and forth   fly out her eyes back in   our tiny bodies float between energy and matter

So this is praise for the point of collision   love desire reckless passion

This is praise for the point of becoming   praise for her ecstasy fearlessness   in us the mice   daisies   comets   the gases of creation Praise for the violence and peace of becoming

This is praise for the fear that brings us in and takes us out praise for the fear of flying and flying anyway

Praise for the noisiness of matter
Praise for the sound of becoming   the boom boom boom of birth

Around the Women's Fire

They ask me to lunch at our favourite restaurant
Lisa Frances Janice Sherry Alex
all winter afternoon   dark at four and us still
spilling talk on the cluttered table

The girls   half-women   spend their chatter
sex   dream babies   periods
husbands   lovers   friends
monsters   flying dreams   women things
over and over   she shouldn't marry him
what does she think
did you see what she wore
her dirty rags everywhere

Here they arrange the ceremonies that bind them
together drag out ancient gods   dress them up for magic
kittens in doll clothes

And I   the crone   sit at the edge
(the men are somewhere else   in my past)
blow smoke rings   hum old tunes
my youth I wind up on my hands
a skein of moments I can shape
reshape at will   in the winter sky
planets hurl down light
more beautiful than young women

What I see
girls of my own young fires
time got them   a cat chasing birds
every generation under the moon

Around the women's fire
chewing the fat   eating snow
we merge with seasons at their genesis
disentangle at the end
little bombs mutating the geography
our bodies
the land

Grandma's Stone

by the fire grandma splits the white stone   inside   a curled ammonite ascends its spiral time   she lifts it out and blows   the shell grows grows grows into a horn   inflates the air with melodies   angel voices dance on the pin of our world   swim out of the ammonite   trout in a stream   dolphins in the sea   this is not for the men   not yet   says grandma   now tell me what you see

and we think of all things that float and dance   in water   in air of seeds of snow of smoke   the cries of animals the voices of people   we think of fish   of seals   we think of whales we think of birds of swallows eagles ospreys kestrels hawks of plovers on a beach of gulls of terns   we think of winter days when air sparkles with ice   we think of wind taking up leaves   we think of geese their flying arrows   of mallards coming down to a marsh   we think of cattails bursting in autumn   of dandelions bursting in spring of rain of clouds before a summer storm   oh we think of the shaman's net flung out   of spirits fleeing   we think of northern lights   ghosts glittering   of shooting stars we think of incense the smell of cooked meat rising   we think of light we think of fire of arms raised to the moon   of prayers going up   we think of bees of wasps how they swarm and hum   the bees of our bodies   the buzz of atoms of gamma rays we think of jacob's ladder of the buzzing in our bones our flesh of the hum the smooth float of voices in our throats rising to the stratosphere in song   we think of hoarfrost capturing the arms of trees   we think of dreams ascending   oh we think of all these things of all these things

how the drummer scatters patterns   a hollow stone   an elk skin stretched over bone   we think of the paradigms of metal how they fly apart re-form   we think of the action of fire   hosanna hosanna the ammonite ascends   unfurls

Everything I Knew

At the centre of my days is a fire, it burns away everything I knew. The fire is on a beach but you can't really tell it's night you see there is only the fire and the night. Sparks fly up to heaven like souls in a drunk saint's vision. I don't really watch, just throw on the wood whatever comes to hand. So I see my arm swing a piece of wood on the fire its orange flames tipped with blue. At the centre of everything is this fire I see nothing else. Do you?

And as you zoom closer with your lens or is it mine you might focus on the beach where the fire is built the sand gives way under my feet as I dance back and forth hefting wood into the fire. In the sand you can see bits of bark and soot they drift down as the fire shoots up its sparks. Now pan up a bit everything around the fire is orange and blue the fire my feet my arm perhaps my face if you can get it.

We could stand back and just watch the fire if you like, or we could go in close, sit in its light. We could all take hands and dance. Someone suggests a midnight picnic but the fire is too big for a wiener roast it would eat everything. I said it's an ancient fire so maybe it's just for scrying.

But how will you scry a fire when the art of it was gone before Prometheus long before anyone knew there had been a before a before filled with just such fires and just such nights such magic. How will we scry this fire what could we learn from it anyway. We might just as well try to read the future by the stars and I grant you there are people who still know how to do that but really what good is it? The future is never the future, it's just a bouquet of probabilities and you can pull any flower out of it you like.

Some people don't like probability some people like the inevitable they like things cast in stone it makes them feel safe. In vain might one point out that even stone changes even stone was once something else: a dinosaur, a tree, lava, sand, you name it. Whole forests become stone, whole beaches, whole skeletons of fish, huge lumps of resin.

Once perhaps several times the whole world was warm there was fire in the air everywhere there was fire close to the ground perhaps it was those great hot piles of dinosaur shit each one the size of a hummock a hillock heating up the atmosphere making horsetail grass grow to the size of sequoias.

Or maybe it was the heat from their rotting bodies. If you had a heat sensor what a field of fire you would find there an aura of orange and blue. And the plants and animals the little ones waiting in the wings did they dream an ice age the excellence of snow the fresh cold air was it they who dreamed together under the blanket of that heat, of mammoth and muskox knee deep in snow snorting steam from their nostrils their breath shooting out then hanging in the air? Was it they who first saw the white bear lift himself from frigid water onto an ice floe steam rising from his wet transparent fur; all this and more dreaming in the orange heat of dinosaur debris.

What was time to them after all they knew once dreamed it would happen it was programmed into their genes into the molecular structure of the universe now and forever amen.

How could they set a future like that like it was set in stone? Believe me when I tell you it was just a probability a white flower picked from the orange and blue bouquet.

And just who dreamed the fires of volcanoes of meteors and comets fire and ice who dreamed all that? Well look at us as we sit and stare into this fire on the beach our bonfire by the evening lake the sun just now dying in its own orange light at the event horizon the west the beautiful west. We ourselves dream volcanoes fire leaping out of mountains slagging down stone. We dream the meteors and comets as the wood of our bonfire pops and shoots out stars of cinder and soot that scream across the night beach hissing into the dark blue lake.

Someone will argue but that's magic and yes of course it is creation is always magic, isn't that grand? Doesn't god always have fun? And how many gods sit at this fire with us as we stir and watch, watch and stir, as we reach over and toss on another log another bundle of sticks?

The Fire in Her Hands

I make a mark on the ground of your mind   A circle in the dirt   stones set round you   You're in a cave   its crystal walls slippery with light   We are inside memory   it plays like movies on the walls   Look up the chimney   see stars like stations of the cross   stones on a field   You want to go out   tumble   another field to dance in   arabesque as though you are in water   no breath   no breathing

This cave then where sky comes down the chimney   we sit here   fire and movies on the walls   There's a hag in the corner   If she turns her face will burn you   Watch her gestures   There pointing there   an old tree   a child playing in the dirt   That's you   she tells you   waiting to be born

Note the child's hands   sticky with resin   twisting twigs   Little hands like insects skittering over the water of a life

She points and points   That's the world   child says   The world   Hag laughs   a circle in the dirt   she says   your place where spirit meets your tailbone   she says   child laughs

Are you still with me?   This cave is an observatory   a womb   a circle in the dirt   The heavens slide down its walls   imprison stars   You can't get out   Breathe hard   The child is playing in a fire

Your hands slip into hers   She puppets you   puts sparks to fingertips   plays them   quarks in a polka   Child is you   says Hag   Child is you waiting to be born

Her little fat hands are ambered with resin and fire   She's making trees   says Hag   She makes snake eyes   bird eyes   flings them at the heavened walls   She puppets   you burn your fingers on your fear   the fire in her hands